The Natural History

of

Stuck-Up People

BY

ALBERT SMITH.

PROFUSELY ILLUSTRATED

BY

GAVARNI, HENNING, AND GILBERT.

LONDON:
WARD AND LOCK, 158, FLEET STREET.

PRYOR PUBLICATIONS
WHITSTABLE AND WALSALL

MEMBER OF
INDEPENDENT PUBLISHERS GUILD

©1995 Pryor Publications

75 Dargate Road, Yorkletts, Whitstable,
Kent CT5 3AE, England.
Tel. & Fax: (01227) 274655
Specialist in Facsimile Reproductions.

ISBN 0 946014 39 6

A CIP Record for this book is available from the British Library.

First Published 1847

Printed and bound by
Biddles Ltd.

Woodbridge Park Estate,
Woodbridge Road,
Guildford GU1 1DA

ALBERT SMITH

Albert Smith, author of 'The Natural History of Stuck-Up People', was one of the greatest showmen of the 19th century. For almost a decade, his entertainments at the Egyptian Hall in Piccadilly were as popular a feature of the capital as Madame Tussaud's and the Tower of London. 'Mr Albert Smith's Ascent of Mont Blanc', his most spectacular show, ran for two thousand performances and earned him thirty thousand pounds. It depicted his actual, and much-publicised, ascent of the mountain.

A considerable figure in the literary and theatrical circles of early Victorian London, the dramas, burlesques and extravaganzas of this extraordinary character were frequently performed, his novels were popular and he was passionately interested in ballooning — although he nearly lost his life when a balloon he was in burst, and came down quicker than it went up.

Albert Smith roused violent feelings in his contemporaries. Some loved him, others detested him. He was not a gentleman — only a bohemian — and the enmity between bohemians and gentlemen culminated in the famous Garrick Club affair when Smith took a stand with Dickens against Thackeray and his supporters.

Born in 1816, he travelled the world widely from his days as a medical student in the Latin Quarter of Paris to his final years in London, where he died in 1860.

Pryor Publications wish to thank *Old Town Books* of Clapham, London for their assistance in the publication of this book.

PREFACE.

WHAT do you mean by "Stuck-up People?" was a question we were asked scores of times, when our little friend the Ballet-girl first carried forth the announcement of the subject on her back, to the reading world.

We hope that in the following pages will

be found a clear explanation of the term—one
that, had we cared to use a French title, might
have been expressed pretty aptly by *Parvenu*.
We do not intend to be particularly funny in
working out our notion : authors who are always
straining to be so. become at last as great
nuisances as people who have always got
" something rather good" to tell you.   We are
alone about to expose, as simply and truthfully
as we can, the foolish conventionalities of a
large proportion of the middling classes of the
present day, who believe that position is attained
by climbing up a staircase of money-bags.

We purpose, then, to further this end by
showing up a purse-proud family of our acquaintance, with whom many of our readers
may have before been upon terms of familiarity

in their own circle; or in a periodical to which we once introduced them. Yet, understand us: we are not about to drag forward any private individuals upon the platform of our public exhibition, for such a proceeding we have ever shrunk from. Nor are we going to sneer at wealth, or the institutions of society— very far from it. Both are excellent things in their way. But we wish to attack the tinselled automata— the brilliant wet blankets, who form what the stuck-up world at present calls "stylish connexions." We mean the members of those coteries, who, located in Belgravia or "Tyburnia," are found either struggling to outdo each other, or all giving in to the whims of one particular individual: like so many geese, following one pertinacious old gander to a pond, where they do not seem to care much about the water, but think they must go because he leads.

These good people, in fine, partake largely of the nature of mushrooms—inasmuch as they have not only sprung up with great rapidity to their present elevation, but have also arisen from mould of questionable delicacy. But now they have no more to do with their former position than has the white button-like fungus in the pottle of the west-end fruiterer with the impure soil from which it drew its vitality

THE NATURAL HISTORY

OF

'STUCK-UP' PEOPLE.

CHAPTER I.

OF THE 'STUCK-UP' FAMILY GENERALLY.

THE head of the family, whose natural history we are about to put forth, is Mr. Spangle Lacquer. He is reported to have made a great deal of money somehow or another, but in what precise way is not known: and he

B

has passed through the three degrees of comparison appropriated to commercial wealth, in the stages of shopkeeper, tradesman, and merchant. He prefers an uncomfortable house at an enormous rent in the Hyde Park division of the Blue Book to any of the most eligible mansions he could command for half the sum in a less fashionable part of the town, because stylish persons live there, and he may be taken for one of them. Mrs. Spangle Lacquer is a very fine lady. She dresses by the fashion-books, believing *berthe* and birth to be words of equal worth in the world, and has reserved seats at all fashionable morning concerts: indeed were she not to be seen at M. Benedict's, she would not hold up her head for the season afterwards.

She has also a pew in a very fashionable church, where religion is made a medium for the display of bonnets in the interior and liveries at the doors: and where some theological partisanship is supported by the clergyman,

who puts on a black robe when he ought to wear a white one; or turns one way when he reads instead of another; or has an altar built out from the wall instead of into it; or performs other antics so well calculated to shake the faith of all in our sublime national creed, when

they see that upon such almost contemptible
points does its holy purity appear to depend.

The young lady Lacquers are immature
daguerreotypes of their mother. Their names
are Emily and Elizabeth, which they spell, at
the end of notes, "Emilie" and "Bessie." They
talk much of the Opera and "the Gardens"
during the season; and never go out shopping

without a page at their heels, except when in their carriage.

As all the world knows the Lacquers have a barouche, of course there is no degradation in their sometimes honouring the earth with their step, with the aforesaid page behind them. Otherwise, the attendance of the retainer is a gloomy piece of poor importance: it always seems to express—" We would keep a carriage if we could."

Young Mr. Lacquer is a specimen of the gentlemanly gent. He haunts the thoroughfares of the west end, and calls his lodgings " cham bers :" his other peculiarities we shall hereafter allude to. The whole family, having a large connexion, are perpetually visiting and receiv ing company—not from any gratification they themselves derive from society, but because they think such laborious indefatigability neces- sary, in following up the most approved precepts of fashion, to enable them to retain their position amidst the crowd of people which they call the World.

These, then, are our acquaintances, with whom, as we have stated, we are particularly intimate: and whose domestic economy we are about to unfold

CHAPTER II.

~~~~~

OF THE LACQUERS' DRAWING-ROOM.

OUR friends the Lacquers reside in a very fashionable part of town, and affect to know nothing of the commercial districts of London. This is the more remarkable, because Mr. Lacquer amassed his gold in those less favoured localities, from soap, bones, tallow, rags, or something equally interesting, by a process of alchemy, which leaves all the old philosophers far behind. But of course all this is scarcely ever recollected by their friends, who, on first

making their acquaintance, are so dazzled
by their display, that they are, for a time, blind
to everything beyond it, until their eyes get
accustomed to the glare, when they recover
their usual vision; and sometimes look deeper
than they ought. For artificial display is
dangerous to have anything to do with, and
resembles a Chinese firework—very flashy and
bewildering at first sight, but if kept up too
long its coruscations are found to proceed only
from the revolutions of a few bits of coloured
transparent paper shining with a borrowed light.

The house in which the Lacquers reside is,
as old Pepys would say, "pleasant to behold,"
and the street door appears to have put on
a suit of brass armour—there being plates of
the visitor's bell, and the servant's bell, and the
kitchen bell, as well as the family name of the
Lacquers, and a command that you will "ring
also," and a notification of the slit for "letters;"
with other amusing and ornamental tablets—

possibly for the purpose of being spelt for
entertainment whilst you are waiting—until the
door resembles a trunk-maker's display of pat-
tern plates.   All these things, however, the
Lacquers look upon as great improvements
upon the habit of our forefathers, in whose
time the only way to get into a house was
simply to knock at the door.   An old lady, a
friend of ours also, who lives opposite—a
simple quiet body, whose idea of enjoying life
consists in sitting at the window for a certain
time every day in a grand cap, and watching
her neighbours—has informed us that whichever
bell you ring the same person always appears
to answer it.   So that the whole process resembles that gone through with the toy used
to gamble with for small gingerbread buttons
at fairs, where you pull strings, and a doll's
head pops up from a hole with a number on it ;
and where, on each attempt to improve your
luck, the same puppet always rises, and never

with the largest number. We have therefore
come to the conclusion that these various bells
have for their object, not so much the division
of labour amongst the domestics, as to an-
nounce to the inmates when any one is going
to make a call—a sort of prompter's signal to
" clear," which means that they must get into
their places and dispose of all unseemly proper-
ties before the drama begins. And this leads us
to give an excellent piece of advice. Whenever you make a morning call at a house, never,
inadvertently, or with the air of a careless
lounger, turn up the sofa cushions, or you will
be certain to make both yourself and your
friends uncomfortable, by the unexpected display of some *mal-a-propos* object or another
that " those tiresome children must have
hidden there."

Having determined, after much careful in-
vestigation, which bell you are to pull, you are
presently admitted by a footman. But as it is

too much trouble for that domestic to go up to the drawing-room with you, he walks to the end of his beat, at the foot of the staircase, and there gives you in charge to another domestic, in whose company you ascend. Arrived at the drawing-room, the footman gives you a chair, pokes the fire, puts some coals on, clatters the fire-irons, tells you his mistress will be down directly, and leaves you to your own meditations.

In walking about the drawing-room at the Lacquers, the chief rule to be observed is to keep your coat-tails under your arm (as Alfred walked with Dorinda through the flower-garden in Bewick's old wood illustration to *The Looking Glass*—a good book rapidly becoming extinct) for fear of knocking over the curiosities crowded into the apartment. There are such wonders of nature and art displayed upon every practicable point of furniture, that the room is a concentrated essence of Wardour Street and Howell and James's. The card-bowl is the

first object your eye falls on· it is of china;
with one or two gilt
doves round it, who are
hopelessly trying to
drink the pasteboards.
The card-bowl is ar-
ranged with much care, for the inspection
of visitors, although with an apparent indif-
ference. The wedding-cards, if the originals
of them chance to be respectable persons, are
placed at top; the best sounding "At Homes"
next; the "Return Thanks"
and "P. D. A.'s" under-
neath; and the small visiting connexions burrow
down at the bottom, in proper retirement.

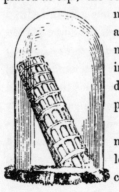

The ornaments are in-
numerable There is a
leaning tower of Pisa, of
course, brought all the way

from there; and a French clock surmounted

by an Ariadne, which young Lacquer insists is taken from the original in the Walhalla of Leicester Square, although his mother is constantly begging and praying that he will not allude to those dreadfully low places, adding, that they saw the original at Frankfort; " Don't you remember, my dear, the day we dined with Mr. Koch?" to the table of which excellent gentleman, somehow or the other, they contrived to wriggle.

Then there is the Prie-dieu chair, which the Miss Lacquers worked all by themselves, in

Berlin wool; but woe betide you if you sit on it; and there are cups, and saucers, and miniatures; inkstands, handbells, and *papier-mâché* nothing-cases, enough to start a bazaar. Some of the curiosities are not very pretty, but worth

a great deal of money, which is not an uncommon attribute of ugliness generally.

But the chief amusement for the morning visitor in waiting is Miss Lacquer's album, which lies on the table amidst some showily-bound religious books. It is a very gorgeous affair, with light pink, and light green, and light blue, and buff, and tea-coloured pages—a literary drawing-room rat-trap, which no one dares to peep into without being caught to pay a visit to his Parnassus. Then there are such sweet rice-paper blue butterflies, all with curved antennæ; and such lovely tinted peacocks and birds of paradise, such shells and seaweed, and singular fuschias— such Byron Beauties, Shakespere Heroines, and Flowers of Loveliness; and such a beautiful gipsy on the first page, begging for scraps, that it is quite refreshing to think there are still such lovely *Bohémiennes* in the world. And the literary portion of this costly book is very pretty indeed. There are the celebrated lines beginning, " Black eyes most dazzle at a ball," written with a crow-quill; and there is also a view of the Bridge of Sighs, done on the middle of a perforated card, with the stanzas underneath

" I stood at Venice,"

which the writer, be sure, never did in his or her life, nor was ever likely to. There are also some verses about " a Moss Rose " underneath a charming flower-painting-taught-in-six-lessons specimen; and an affecting sonnet " Upon hearing an infant sneeze in its sleep." There are, besides, some lines about " My little foot-page," which are whispered as the production of Miss Lacquer herself, but which do not mean the small boy in buttons attached to the establishment; and many other excellent *morçeaux* tending in the highest degree to assist genteel reason and refined reflection. And there is a fashionable drawing-room ballad, written by Miss Lacquer, and composed by her music-master, after the style of a celebrated modern lyric poet, which we here subjoin :—

BALLAD FROM A MS. GRAND OPERA.

" WHEN FOND AFFECTION."

When fond affection's memory flings
   Her ivied mantle o'er the past,
And grief its calm reflection brings
   To vanished hopes o'er bright to last;

One word alone should then be spoken,
  One word alone the soul can tell,
By which e'en hollow hearts are broken,
  The lingering murmur—Fare-thee-well !

When happiness in gilded wear
  Shall mask the cheek with transient smiles,
And lighten up life's landscape drear
  With tales of love and beauty's wiles;
What still is in the power of words
  The deep love of the heart to tell ?
It is the harp's sad dying chords,
  The lingering murmur—Fare-thee-well !

Then there is a great admirer of Alfred
Tennyson who hath perpetrated the following—
imitation being the sincerest flattery :—

LADY VIOLET VAVASOUR.

Lady Violet Vavasour,
  For me you need not keep a stall ;
You thought to get my five-pound note,
  And give no change, but keep it all.

But though I came prepared to buy,
    I saw the snare and I retired ;
A wool-worked mat, at such a price,
    Is not a thing to be desired.

Lady Violet Vavasour,
    You put strange fancies in my head,
Since twice, at Lady Harclay's ball,
    You all but waltzed young Howard dead.
Oh ! your small feet—your deux-temps fleet,
    Most fascinating you may be,
But such a fright you made him look,
    That you had hardly cared to see.

Lady Violet Vavasour,
    You pine amidst your pasteboard towers,
Your drawings, autographs, and lace,
    Your slippers, purses, and wax flowers,
For that bright Blonde sells more than you :
    There, lay that five-pound urn-mat down,
And give me that pincushion heart,
    Too dearly bought at half-a-crown.

The above lines were written by a young
barrister after a fancy-fair at which the Lacquers
assisted, and to which we shall presently refer.

Miss Lacquer had at one time no very great notion of Tennyson, having heard he was simply natural—and consequently common-place—in his poetry: but since she had seen his works at a great house she called at (we all know the "great house" of our connexions) she had become one of his devoted admirers. And when she at last heard that the Queen admired his writings, she became wild in her enthusiasm: and was always wishing that she were the Queen o' the May to be called early.

The same contributor played her album a sad trick. He promised to procure her a poem by Mr. Monckton Milnes, which quite overcame Miss Lacquer, as she had seen that gentleman's name so often at leading *réunions* ("amongst the company present" that the *Post* noticed) that she was sure he must be a nice poet. But her young friend sent back the album with these verses, which somewhat puzzled her as to their authenticity:—

c 2

THE LONG-AGO.

In the antique dealer's store,
    Precious chairs and tables sleep,
Which were not, in days of yore,
    E'er considered worth their keep;
Cupboards that are cupboards still
    Into cabinets can grow;
Nothing's altogether ill
    If it was made long-ago.

Hazy glass that scarcely shines,
    Tenement of by-gone beers,
Looks as made for costly wines,
    Through the mist of hazy years.
Bad utensils turn to good,
    Old books are no longer slow;
Oh! we would not, if we could,
    Disbelieve in long-ago.

Though the doom of swift decay
    Shocks the soles of patent boots;
Though the seediness of age
    Quickest comes on cheapest suits:

Still the boots will be forgotten,
　We shall think not on the blow,
Never grieve o'er paletots rotten,
　If the past be long-ago.

There are many other pieces of poetry: together with laconics extracted from good authors: such as—

" In being asked for our autograph there is something gratifying to our vanity, provided it be not on the back of a bill."
ROCHEFOUCAULT.

and similar ones. But we have been looking over the album so long that we have quite forgotten the owners, to whom we now turn our attention.

CHAPTER III.

OF THE YOUNG LADIES, AND LACQUER BENEVO LENCE IN GENERAL.

WE HAVE mentioned, *en passant*, the young lady Lacquers: we will now endeavour to make the reader better acquainted with them. These young ladies, then, feel great pleasure in stating that they "were never at school;" and Mrs. Lacquer has an honest pride in avow ing that, thank God, her daughters were brought up at home, solely from the idea that it was the only way of producing pure-minded and well-educated young women. Those narrow-minded people who affect to sneer at Mrs. Lacquer, for that display which they can never hope to compass, affirm that there were other reasons for domestic tuition. In fact that, because when her daughters were growing up there were several more in family, it was deemed cheaper to work to death a talented and broken-hearted girl, as governess, in instructing the whole party at once, than to place them separately at some school.

So have we seen, at taverns, five people club together their shillings for the luxury of a bowl of punch, and be looked upon for a while as the heads of the room, where, otherwise they would have been compelled to be content with single measures of plebeian spirits. So do passengers in the street throw forth their united halfpence to command the exertions of the famishing mountebank, whose performance they could not have commanded for themselves alone.

The governess of the young lady Lacquers taught them a useful lesson beyond the ordi-

nary routine of tuition, inculcating a proper
pride of station, and the importance of money
She was far superior to them both in family
and acquirements.   Her father's crest had
never needed to be " found" by ingenious seal-
engravers of inventive minds: for she knew
that her ancestors had borne it on their shields
at Agincourt.   But the Lacquers were enabled,
through their excellent bringing-up, to look upon
her merely as a superior domestic—the *entresol*
in their architectural scale of society; and they
regarded her with a perfect absence of that awk-
ward feeling which would certainly have affected
low people.   And, of course, the mere fact of their
so constantly and studiously endeavouring to
make the governess perfectly aware of what she
was, proved that they thought nothing of her.

The Misses Lacquer are now perfectly ac-
complished, masters having perfected what the
governess left undone.   Common French they
look upon as their own tongue, bringing it in,

both in writing and speaking, wherever they
can; but it is wonderful to hear them talk
German—even the very natives of that country
have been amazed at it. Emily has, of course,
translated Burger's *Lenore*, and Bessie has
illustrated it with a copy of Vernet's ghastly

picture in this manner, which is pronounced to
be superior to the original.   And the manner
in which, when they show it, they both quote

" Graut Liebchen auch? der Mond scheint hell!
    Hurrah! die Todten reiten schnell!
    Graut Liebchen auch vor Todten?"
" Ach, nein! doch las die Todten!"

is pronounced by listeners to be truly awful.

Their knowledge of Italian is so perfect,
they would not, for the world, be seen with a
book at the Opera.   They would as soon think
of singing an English ballad in society, unless
they smothered up the words and overlaid the
air with roulades, so that by thus stifling the
original song altogether, nobody could exactly
tell what it was.

They have a great idea of the Horticultural
Fête, at Chiswick, and are usually to be met
with at all three; although they give it out
generally that they only go to the middle one.

They feel great gratification when their carriage
draws up at the gate, before the people who are
waiting for their own equipages. They could
get in much sooner, and far more comfortably,
by walking down to where it was waiting at the
side of Turnham Green; but then nobody would
see its gaudy liveries and conspicuous heraldic
bearings. Once they found it necessary to
cut a friend of their brother's because he had
the temerity, in the open face of a beautiful
July day, calmly and deliberately, to go from
Hyde Park Corner to Chiswick on the roof of
an omnibus; and, what was worse, smile at
them when he met them. But this ultra-
propriety does not always appear; for Bessie
Lacquer does not mind being driven down
through the park by the Honourable Such-a-one,
of the Blues, upon his assurance to her mamma
that he will take every care of her; and her
mamma's assurance to him, in return, that she
would not let Bessie go with anybody else;

which is remarkable, when the gallant gentleman's popular reputation is considered. To do
the Lacquer girls justice, they are very hand-
some; just that style of effective beauty that
men like to be seen with. They are of the
order of girls who know the household army
list by heart, and believe greatly in military
men; girls, whom all agree to be glorious in a

ball-room, or at a fête, but whom so few think
of marrying.

And yet people expect the Lacquer girls
will make eligible matches. They have been
" out " four or five seasons—for as the high-born
daughters of England keep up that ceremony
of inauguration into the mysteries of the Hy-
meneal Stock Exchange, the Lacquers must do
the same: they have not gone off yet, it is
true, but they will do so. Envious report,
however, says that there is very little money
attached to them; that whilst old Lacquer is
very rich, still other expenses are proportionally
great, and that all they can look forward to,
will be what he leaves—not what he gives
them. And yet this is scarcely just, for Mr.
Lacquer's liberality and benevolence are at-
tested by every printed subscription—the true
charity that relieves those proper objects whose
distress is publicly heralded forth by a phalanx
of important names, in preference to the swin

dling whinings of pitiful unknown hearts that
burst in seclusion. Does an hospital require
to be built, or an infirmary or asylum to be
established, Mr. Lacquer's open hand immediately comes down with fifty or a hundred
pounds. Is there an eleemosynary sermon at a
fashionable church, the gold glitters in the sun-
light as Mr. Lacquer drops it into the plate so
accommodatingly presented to him : but he
never encourages illness or want by covertly
aiding the same individuals for whom the
charity is founded that he has assisted to endow

Mrs. Lacquer has precisely the same right-
minded feeling; and with it she combines true
hospitality and the desire to do honour to her
guests. For when she holds a grand *réunion*,
such as we may presently speak more fully of,
she does not care how many wax candles blaze
in the branches and chandeliers of the apartments for the gratification of the company.
We say the gratification of the company, be-

cause it is evident that this single-minded
woman dislikes such show. We know this from
having one evening dropped in by chance, when
nobody was there, nor indeed expected, and found
her with a solitary metallic wick, reading as she
best might. And we have heard from discarded
servants that the *menu* of the dinner was sometimes rather scanty when it was a mere family
meal; that they did not even then use the covers
" with handles to take off and form dishes,"
which they appeared, at their dinner-parties,
to consider as belonging to a service of the
most every-day kind. But these are reports
which we really blush to chronicle, when we
reflect upon the quarter from whence they are
derived.

Mais revenons a—pshaw! that hacknied
sentence is quite worn out in the service of a
species of literary police, in bringing back run-
away subjects to their proper place, so we will
not use it but discard it henceforth We meant

it to imply that we were about to return to the
Misses Lacquer. Their admiration of the
plants at the botanical exhibitions is guided
entirely by who is looking at them too. A
giant Cactus, in itself, would be characterised
as " a frightful great thing," but if it attracts

the attention of any nice persons, and especi
ally an officer, the Lacquer girls admire the
fine specimen of the Cactus so intensely, that
it is impossible to get them away from the tub;
and the glow of enthusiasm that lights up their
faces, turned towards the intended bystander,
as they exclaim "How superb! how splendid!"
is delightful to contemplate.

Next to the Horticultural Fête, and perhaps
Kensington Gardens, the great effects in dress
and appearance are economised for the au-
tumnal visit to the sea-side; whither the
Lacquers always migrate, and remain, while
there, in a fashionable expensive boarding-
house. Their chief amusement here is carry-
ing on a matrimonial game of chess, as soon as
they become assured of the actual great expec-
tations of any bachelor therein residing They
have several times met with such a one, and
endeavoured, by chasing him about the squares
and constantly giving him check, to compel him

to take them. Up to the present time they
have not succeeded, from want of proper finesse,
although they leave London every year with the
rest of the world. Indeed of such vital importance is this migration, that one season when
they were compelled to stay in town, Mrs.
Lacquer and her daughters never left the house,
but papered up the blinds, tied up the chande-
lier, and shut the shutters of the front rooms;
living for six weeks in the back apartments
overlooking the dead wall of the mews.

CHAPTER IV.

OF THE GENERAL SOCIETY MET AT THE LACQUERS

OUR friends the Lacquers have two distinct sets of acquaintances—those whom they knew formerly in the city, and those that have been introduced to them since they set up their west-end establishment; and as these two parties do not very well harmonize,

the greatest skill and management is necessary
to prevent any uncomfortable collisions. And
so their assemblies are always the result of
much careful arrangement, except the large
balls, where, owing to the crowded state of the
rooms, anybody can pass muster tolerably well,
from the mercantile friends of former times, to
the semi-unproducible relations of the present
day, whom it is found necessary to cut dead in
the park, if the Lacquers are riding with any
of their high connexions. But these latter
persons, being low and uncivilized, think that
consanguinity is a sufficient plea for intimacy;
and are always calling just when they ought
not, in consequence of which attention the
Lacquers give them a set dinner annually, "to
keep up old feelings and natural affection," as
Mr. Lacquer always says on these occasions.
The period fixed for these *réunions* is generally
as much out of the season as it can be, because
the semi-unproducibles are always happy to

accept the invitation of the Lacquers at any
time; and the early close of day veils the
motley train of hack vehicles which, according
to the usual habits of vulgar people, always
arrive together at the door within a minute of
the exact time.

Several distinguished foreigners—chiefly
counts and barons—are usually met with at
the Lacquers' great parties, and then the
hostess addresses them in a louder tone than
ordinary, and by their titles. The greater
part of the company know them very well in
Regent Street, or rather think they do; for
most distinguished foreigners so resemble
one another, that we ourselves sometimes
imagine that we have seen the Lacquers'
friends in the most questionable haunts in
London; but this must be a mistake—such
imposing specimens of alien aristocracy would
never have stooped to visit the places in
question. The Baron Devoidoff Witz is the

most popular of the Continentalists. He is a
rollicking young cavalier of eight-and-forty, who
finds much favour in the eyes of the young
ladies, by giving out that he has a large fortune,
and is looking after a wife; and so he is usually

seen with one of the best girls in the room upon
his arm. *Au reste*, he is harmless, which is
much more than can be said of the majority of
distinguished foreigners who glitter in the
parvenu drawing-rooms of our great London.
They all speak English with tolerable accuracy,
but the Misses Lacquer think it good breeding
to keep up a conversation with them in their
own language.

After a time some of these illustrious
persons disappear and are heard of no more;
others re-appear rather too prominently, and
are heard of a great deal too much; and others
again, perhaps the majority, may be met, when
the season has passed, in the secluded back
settlements of the towns of Kentish and
Camden—spots which find peculiar favour, as
far as regards cheap rustication, in the eyes of
the million unshaven foreign adventurers, who
swarm over here annually for the sake of
swindling their way into decent society, or

robbing poor John Bull in the impudent manner which that worthy gentleman so very quietly puts up with.

If you mention any one of these latter migratory beings, the Lacquers will always tell you that it is not the same person whom you have met at their house. Possibly not: yet with all their aristocratic bearing we have sometimes trembled for the spoons when we have narrowly watched two or three of these stars at the parties. And the Lacquers afford greater room for this fear from their tables being always loaded with plate. But this is a point of economy after all: for people are not in the habit of devouring silver forks and candle-sticks, and they cost nothing to keep when not in use: whilst with their aid a very little refreshment goes a great way. Six brandy-cherries in the branch of an *epergne* become prominent portions of the feast, when they would have been passed over in a saucer of cheap blown glass or a pickle dish. The large vase of artificial flowers at the top—which, like the wreath of Dr. Parr's maypole, is carefully put by when the fête is over, to come out again in undiminished glory at the next—does away with the trifle by occupying its place, and looks more imposing. The small mould of cream is aggrandized by the heavy moulding of the dish on which it is placed; and throughout the whole banquet the same evidences appear of the *economy of splendour*. Indeed the endeavour to pick out something slightly substantial, reminds one of Sindbad hunting for food in the Valley of Diamonds before the merchants above threw down the legs of mutton. Equally with the Lacquers, are Greenwich and Blackwall tavern-keepers aware of the power of plated dishes in increasing the importance of the viands they contain : or three or four pieces of stewed eel would never pass muster. as they do, in the eyes of the hungry guest who has just quitted the river—to say nothing of salmon cutlets and *filets de sole*.

The young men who frequent the Lacquers' house, keep cabs, and talk largely of their winnings at cards, and their clubs (although you cannot distinctly understand to which they belong), and the men they know in the guards. Without being regularly sporting-men, they assume a great knowledge of dogs, and horses, and the state of the odds. Young Lacquer, from associating with them, insensibly—insensibly enough—falls into their style of conversation, and speaks about "making up his book" as a matter of great moment: although it is believed by ordinary common-minded persons that a five-pound note would at any time cover his speculations, whichever way luck might turn. He is, at present, keeping his terms in the Temple: and sometimes honours those whom he considers the more eligible of his fellow-students with invitations to his house;

where, following the custom of unweaned
barristers generally in after-dinner society,
they differ in opinion with everybody at table
for the sake of knocking up an argument: and
this is kept up with great powers of contradic-
tion, in proportion to the perfectly unimportant
nature of the subject, and to the great delight
and edification of the other guests. Mr
Lacquer never joins much in the conversation
unless it relates to money or capital; and then
he appears to be so very humorous and entertaining, that his visitors are continually laugh-
ing at him. Sometimes, to be sure, a slight
trip in his grammar carries back the mind of
his auditor to the days of his early education,
but he is not courted one whit the less upon
this account. His money brings position, and
position brings influence; and he enjoys the
high gratification of affording room for his acquaintances to place his skull far beneath his
breeches' pocket, in point of value as to what it

contains. For gold is the best joker in the world : its sallies always tell.

You will always be certain to meet at the Lacquers' a great many persons with whom you are perfectly well acquainted by sight, but to whom you can assign no fixed position in society, having generally met them in places where distinction was acquired by paying for it. You will see them sailing up the avenues of a morning concert to the reserved seats ; they cross your pathway in going to their carriages from Howell and James's ; they brush against you at the conclusion of the performances at the Opera ; and they put their faith in Gunter, firmly believing that his ice is much colder than even that of Wenham Lake—at all events it is expensive, which, placing it more out of the power of the common-place million, must of course endow it with superior attributes of some kind or another. It is this eligible class that forms the great proportion of Mrs. Lac-

quer's visiting acquaintance just at present,
and the continual struggle between them all
to outdo the others in display is most amusing.
The feeling extends to the younger branches—
especially the girls; if any of them even appear in the parks on a finer horse than their

acquaintances, the Lacquers never let their father rest until they also have one equally conspicuous: indeed Bessie will, without doubt, have an elephant before long, sooner than be outdone.

All this fighting, either in anticipating the others in some expensive novelty for the table or palate, or in the matter of dress or show-off, proves that they work harder, and experience many more cutting vexations, than the nobodies of the middling circles who do not enjoy a twentieth part of their income; but who nevertheless contrive occasionally, to the extraordinary astonishment of Mrs. Lacquer and her friends, to get into a particular sphere of society which they, with all their dash and expenditure, are unable to accomplish.

CHAPTER V

A DINNER-PARTY AT THE LACQUERS'

HAVING introduced our readers to the Spangle Lacquers, and some of their connexions, we will now reunite them at a dinner-party given by this superior family. Or rather we will attempt to do so; for it is difficult to write through music, and an attendant demon of annoyance is beneath our window playing the Post-horn Gallop very slowly, on an organ, and chirping an accompaniment to it on a bird-whistle, more or less in a different key. So—he is gone to worry the neighbours at last, and we may now proceed.

Those accustomed to mix in society upon whose opinion we can rely, have decided that dinner-parties originated in remote ages from a desire on the part of the giver to collect around him those friends in whose society he felt the greatest pleasure. But time effects singular changes, and the Spangle Lacquers, at the present day, in company with many others, appear only anxious to invite those with whom they are constantly sparring for position in the vast arena of fiddle-faddle gentility; entirely forgetting also, that the social observances of the real aristocracy, however proper when confined to the class amongst whom they arose, become pitifully ludicrous in the imitations of second or third rate establishments.

A grand dinner-party at the Lacquers' is a
dreary festival of ostentation; and yet the
guests must think it pleasant and entertaining,
or they would not come. We must confess
that our own ideas of sociability are somewhat
different; but it does not follow that they are
right, nor would we have them considered the
standard of general opinion in consequence.

As we are in the habit of seeing only one
phase of life, and that an inferior one, we dined
at the Lacquers' a short time ago, having first
studied the *Hints upon Etiquette* for some days
previously, that we might not commit ourselves
by any unpolished action. Half-past six for
seven was the appointed feeding-time; and
about the latter hour we presented ourselves at
the house, and were ushered, with due solemnity,
into the drawing-room. Nobody had yet
assembled beyond the family, who were all
sitting, *en grande tenue*, upon the embroidered
sofas and ottomans, divested for that day of

their chintz skins. The majority of the guests, however, arrived within twenty minutes of the time: and then we heard from each what singular weather it was for the time of year, and how rapidly town was filling. Mrs. Lacquer kept casting such anxious glances at the spidery hands of a large ormolu time-piece, that we saw the whole of the party had not come to their time; and, at about a quarter to eight, Mr. and Mrs. Fitzmoses were ushered into the room, and Mrs. Spangle Lacquer told them how very happy she was to see them— which I believe, at the moment, was the case. We were much amused to hear young Lacquer tell his sister "that the Fitzmoses were not in a position to keep people waiting so long, although they always did it." By this we learnt a custom of which we were before ignorant—that the higher the station people acquire in life, the later they may come to a dinner-party. We have no doubt, allowing

an hour to every degree, that after twenty-four
ascending ranks, supposing it brings us to a
duke, his invitation is always meant to imply
the same hour on the day after that for which
it is given.

After much manœuvring on the part of
Mrs. Lacquer to get the most eligible persons
together, with proper regard to their prece-
dency, we went down stairs in very grave pro-
cession, and finally settled into our respective
places. The brilliancy of the table so dazzled
us, that we have not a distinct recollection of
the first ten minutes, except convulsively swal-
lowing some white soup, which one of the servants appeared to insist upon our tasting. But
when the fish was served, we began to see the
triumph of form over comfort. The plates
were costly, and the devices heraldic, but we
could get no lobster sauce ; the forks were
heavy and richly chased, but the cayenne was
detained at the bottom of the room by the

apparent combination of the footmen. So we ate our two inches of turbot *au naturel*, and made up with bread, pretending that we liked it best in that fashion; indeed, as a dead silence reigned over the table during the entire course, we picked our little French roll entirely to pieces, for the express purpose to appear to be doing something and not feeling uncomfortable. And we looked about the room, especially at the pictures, which were rather

remarkable for the heavy gilding of the frames, than their subjects or style. There were, of course, Mr. and Mrs. Lacquer as large as life, and two Wardour Street ancestors — one, a Charles the Second beauty, being, as

he informed us, his great-great-grandmother,
which, being so, it was rather a wonder he
allowed to remain in an old curiosity shop so
long ; and the other was a quiet old gentleman,
whom we had been told was
Mrs. Lacquer's uncle, but
who, somehow or another,
got into the hands of a family in Surrey, at whose
sale he had been recovered.
Nothing is so easy to set up

as ancestors : and the older the better, because
then nobody can question the likeness.

But with all our endeavours to appear
civilised, we sadly committed ourselves in asking for some beer—a liquid prepared from a
preparation of barley, formerly drunk at dinner,
during the savage state of English society.
We had seen nothing about its impropriety in
the *Hints upon Etiquette*, and had, therefore,
ventured to ask for it—the more so, because

when we once took luncheon with the Lacquers, we saw them all drink a very fair quantity of the outlawed beverage. But when we witnessed the haggard look of the butler upon asking him for it—when we saw Mrs. Lacquer nearly fainting, and the young ladies glancing at us as if we had been the Chinese ambassador, we perceived that we had sunk beyond redemption in their esteem; and for the time, determined never to go into high society again, but enjoy our diurnal pint of stout, or half-and-half, as the case might be, at home. For there are still certain spots in London where the discarded liquid may be obtained; but these are in very low neighbourhoods, which the Lacquers never heard of.

The pageant went on in the ordinary routine of dinner-party solemnity; in which cutlets of grave expression, and patties of aristocratic demeanour, made their appearance, and vanished—there being in company, with the generality of side-dishes, things that nobody ever thinks of taking, and which might be just as well made, for show alone. out of *papier-mâché*. Then, we should have liked a little wine, but no one asked us to take any, and we knew no one near us to ask; besides which, we had a blue glass, and an amethyst-coloured glass, and a broad shallow glass, and a tall glass, and a tumbler: all which varieties exceedingly perplexed us: and we heard afterwards that taking wine with people "had gone out of fashion," but that the servant came round and filled for you. "Out of fashion," pah! away with such twaddle. Taking wine with another person was not a very imposing ceremony, we admit; but it evinced the desire to pay attention to the party challenged, and the wish to exhibit a friendly feeling. It was simply hospitable, and so it is "out of fashion!"

When the pastry made its appearance upon table, there was a little tart, of which Mrs

Lacquer did not know the contents—of course
not, how should she? But we smiled involun-
tarily, as we called to mind an anecdote, which
we will recount for the edification of our readers,
as well as a warning.

A certain lady—one of the Lacquer class,
who will not always bear dropping down upon
to dinner unexpectedly—was one day much
alarmed by the sudden arrival of some hungry
visitors from the country. Knowing that the
carte du jour of her kitchen was not very exten-
sive, she despatched her servant to the nearest
confectioner's for some large tarts (which, by
the way, the Lacquers call *tourtes*). The articles
in question appeared at dinner, and made a
very passable dish; and all would have gone
off very well but for a sudden attempt on the
part of the mistress at conventional show-off.
Wishing to exhibit her ignorance of their contents, she pointed to them, and turning round
to the footman with an air of great dignity,

exclaimed, "John—what are these tarts?"
Whereat John, in the innocence of his heart,
looking at the tarts in a commercial, rather
than a culinary point of view, briskly replied,
"Fourpence a piece, ma'am."

CHAPTER VI.

~~~~~~

A DINNER-PARTY AT THE LACQUERS'

(CONTINUED.)

As the Lacquers are very fond of crowding as many expensive things upon the table as possible, in the display of which they think society consists; and as they look more for the dash of equipage than the brilliancy of intellect in their acquaintances, we readily anticipated what the after-dinner part of the entertainments would resemble. Everything was in the extreme of dreary splendour. The orange chips were from Gunter's—the preserves from Fortnum and Mason's—whilst the dessert service was a blaze of enamelled gold, all which being arranged in solemn state, Mrs. Lacquer thought that the great end of giving a dinner-party was obtained. There was that public profusion which, amongst the Lacquer species, always accompanies private economy—that ostentatious extravagance ever inseparable from domestic parsimony. We never see this show-off style of living, but we imagine that the servants must fare indifferently. And indeed it has been whispered to us that Mrs. Lacquer weighs out half a pound of butter every week to each of the domestics for their seven days' allowance; that the store-room is a perfect bastile of imprisoned grocery; and that the Misses Lacquers, who, with all their wonderful notions, take the housekeeping by turns, "give out" the small quantities of pepper, nutmeg, and other humble condiments required for the culinary purposes of the family. But this is all very proper, inasmuch as it keeps up the proper line of distinction between superiors and attendants—far more commendable than the habits of some grovelling and mean-spirited people, who allow their servants actually to feed upon the same joint as they themselves are in the habit of dining from—and even without marking off the kitchen allowance.

The ladies did not stay long at table after the dessert had been arranged. Few of them took any wine, and fewer still said a word worth attending to—nearly the whole of their conversation being confined to fiddle-faddle remarks of the most inane description. Several times,

indeed, there was a dead silence—one of those
miserable pauses which are always prolonged
by the wish to think of some common-place
observation that might break it, and which
never comes to your relief when it is most
wanted.   But, pause or not, Mrs. Lacquer still
sat in all the pride of pomp at the head of the
table, thinking that she had done quite enough
towards honouring her guest, by putting on her
emerald velvet dress and point lace, and cover-
ing the table with a costly dessert.   At last,
after a longer pause than ordinary, she collected
all the glances of the ladies' eyes into one focus,
which was herself; and then, by some peculiar
freemasonry, they all rose at once, and sailed
out of the room—an active gentleman in
a white cravat opening the door for them;
and two of the ladies who went out wound
their arms around one another's waists in an
impulse of girlish affection, most refreshing and

delightful to behold—they could neither of
them ever expect to see thirty again.

Mr. Lacquer now moved to the head of the table, and directed his guests to draw up nearer to him, which they did, apparently for the purpose of hearing him relate the history of every separate bottle of wine that came to table, each of which, by his account, was a kind not to be met with every day, but especially procured for him by his friend Logwood, at a great price, with the assurance that he was the only man who could have obtained it. Then the young gentleman, who opened the door, addressed a remark to us concerning some *fracas* in the Jockey Club; but finding we knew nothing about it, passed us over with a glance of contempt, and directly turned his attention to young Lacquer, who, mixing in better society than ourselves, was quite up to all the chicanery of the turf. And next young Lacquer told him, in confidence, of a sweet mare that he tried the other day; and only differed with the owner about a five-pound note, or he should have pur chased her. And then they finally agreed to drive a break along the Edgeware Road the next day, along with some man who knew Paul Bedford, and had got one of Mademoiselle Caroline's gloves which she had given to him herself at Vauxhall; and which lay in state at his rooms every day for fellows to come

and admire and envy. Two or three other guests were hard at work upon Sir Robert Peel and Lord George Bentinck; and one sharp-faced old gentleman was regarding everybody as they spoke with an air of smiling acquiescence and intent interest, that convinced us he was an humble acquaintance, asked at three-quarters past the eleventh hour, to fill up a vacancy, and balance the order of the table. And we were the more certain of this, because at dinner, whenever he was asked which particular portion of any dish he had a fancy to, he always replied, " Any part, any part, thank you; I have no preference—whichever you please." Whenever the conversation came to a standstill, Mr. Lacquer leant back in his chair, jingled his gold in his breeches' pocket, danced his heavy watch-seals in his hand, and asked if any of his friends knew of an eligible investment for fourteen thousand pounds, which he had to spare at present. And if no one responded to this in-

quiry, and the silence continued, he told somebody to take a clean glass and try the claret,
which he could recommend as something rather
out of the common way; or asked if Burgundy
would be preferable, because he had some in his
cellar, and would send for it if required.

And in this manner two or three tedious
hours wore away, until we were summoned, for
the third time, to coffee; when we gladly walked
up stairs, even with the slight promise of entertainment which the drawing-room afforded;
contrasting, in our own mind, the dismal soci-
ality we had just witnessed, in spite of the pine-
apple and chrystallized apricots, with the kind-
heartedness and sparkling conversation which
are never to be met with higher than a couple
of plain decanters with port and sherry, and
some simple English walnuts (or a few filberts
—we especially cling to filberts), and some crisp,
toothsome biscuits

A little formal amusement took place when

we had finished our coffee. The Misses Lacquer played a piece of four-and-twenty pages in

length, for the piano and harp, which threw everybody into ecstasies except ourselves, and afterwards sang *Giorno d'Orrore*, from Semi-ramide, to prove their versatility of talent. The rest of the company sat still and admired, or looked at albums and picturesque annuals— those harbours of refuge for the unamused —which they had seen an hundred times before, until their carriages were ordered, when they disappeared as quietly and imperceptibly as a gradual thaw, with about the same degree of coldness, being but a few degrees above freezing.

As this appeared to be the general style of entertainment which they provided for each other, we were not surprised to hear one or two of the guests express their obligations to Mrs Lacquer for their very pleasant party: but as our own feelings were quite different, we said no such thing, making our escape with much joy, and inwardly resolving to "regret that a previous engagement prevented us from accept-ing Mrs. Spangle Lacquer's polite invitation," should that lady again honour us with one.

CHAPTER VII.

~~~~~

A FANCY-FAIR

CHARITY IT is said, covereth a multitude of sins ; and when she does so with a veil of costly manufacture, however delicate and transparent its texture, the concealment is much more effectual than if it were a tarpaulin of the coarsest sackcloth. The Lacquers are perfectly aware of this, and consequently are never backward in eleemosynary offerings, provided always that the object be a fashionable one, approved of by their set; and that their liberality be not hidden under a bushel, but placarded in great thoroughfares, and proclaimed to the world by the speaking-trumpet of ostentation.

Some little time back, in consequence of embarrassed funds, the patronesses of the "Ladies'-babies'-bib-and-tucker-general-loan-association" determined upon holding a fancy-fair for the benefit of the institution; and were fortunate enough not only to secure the approving countenance of the Dowager Lady Floss for the undertaking, but also to get a sermon preached in its favour by a pet parson at a fashionable church. Our acquaintances were amongst the first applied to for their support, which Mrs. Lacquer cheerfully promised,

saying, " that there was no labour in the world
more gratifying than that of alleviating the
distresses of our fellow-creatures; and that
this had been her principal aim in giving her
daughters the first education money could fur-
nish." And then the patronesses of the association went away rejoicing, and proclaimed
everywhere what kind and benevolent people
the Lacquers were. But we ourselves had
always been accustomed to look upon Mrs.
Spangle Lacquer as a gaudy French clock, with
very inferior works, which might be seen
through the glass sides; and when we regarded
the inward springs that set the motives of her
life in action, we found out, that unless there
had been a chance of her daughters' keeping a
stall, or having their productions lauded and
chronicled in the columns of a fashionable
journal, the " Ladies'-babies'-bib-and-tucker-ge-
neral-loan-association" might have fallen to the
ground with the greatest pleasure in the world

on the part of Mrs. Lacquer. But the fair
was expected to be fashionably attended —
fashionable families gave it their countenance —
the very circumstance of young aristrocratic
ladies lowering themselves to trade, and playing at shop-girls, was fashionable—and very
fashionable company were to be admitted the
first day at half-a-crown a piece for the mere
privilege of entrance. But that the noble
objects of the institution might be universal,
and all allowed to contribute to their further-
ance, common people were allowed to pay a
shilling, and come in on the last day, when
some of the articles began to hang on hand,
and the more select visitors had picked out
what goods most captivated their fancy. What
a blessed and single-hearted feeling is the
charity which manifests itself so openly at
fancy-fairs, and allows every one to exercise
his benevolence !

The Lacquers immediately set to work and

made all sorts of fancy articles; and what they
did not make, they bought at the bazaars, and
sent in under their names, which answered the
purpose just as well. First of all, as they had
been taught drawing, they produced an immense
quantity of fire-screens, adorned with sketches
of what appeared to be aristocratic periwinkle
and whelk shells, reposing on shreds of pink
and blue bird's-eye tobacco, intended, in the
luxuriance of their imaginations, for seaweed;
over which were hovering various unknown
butterflies, with tinsel wings, most appropri-
ately introduced—the butterfly being, as everybody is aware, a marine insect that resides at
the bottom of the sea. Then their grocer was
ordered to send them various grape-jars, painted
green, and furnished with gilt knobs; and
having bought a piece of gaudy chintz at a
leading upholsterers, they cut out all the birds
and flowers imprinted thereon, and stuck them
on the jars, which were subsequently varnished,

and called "Macao Vases." Mrs. Lacquer was not very great in drawing or painting, but she bought bundles of short straws at her bonnet-maker's, and fixing them in circular frames of pasteboard, twisted blue ribbon in and out, making them resemble Lilliputian hurdles; and when the apparatus was complete, it was termed a spill-case, to be sold, with similar ones, at a guinea the pair. And next a quantity of trays of white wood, together with card-cases, envelope-boxes, glove-containers, and many other contrivances of the same material, were laid in from the fashionable stationer's. These were intended to be adorned with the transfer-work; and then what havoc began! Innumerable lithographs were immolated—all the table-covers in the house were varnished, more or less; and the bottles were broken, and corks left out, and contents all evaporated or dried. And the Misses Lacquer themselves, for an entire week, had such very sticky fingers, that the young men of fashion who had the *entrée* of the house, and came to talk captivating nothings to the ladies, or hold their skeins of

silk whilst they were engaged in their fancy manufactures, declared that shaking hands with them was one of the most delightful sensations

which they—the young men of fashion—had
experienced for some time. They were fairly
detained for a minute in the thrilling and
adhesive grasp of the young ladies.

The Misses Lacquer did not do a great deal
in the Berlin-wool line—they pronounced it
worn-out, and too much followed by common
people to create any more sensation. Possibly
they might have thought that it was a great
deal of trouble with a very little effect—but
this by the way. But they performed some
very curious feats of sleight of hand, with a
pack of perforated cards, torturing them into
sticking-plaster cases, and what-nots ; and when
their ingenuity could devise no fresh shape to
stitch them into, they turned their attention
to the perforations themselves, and pushed
needles, followed by trains of coloured floss
silk, through the little round holes, which they
termed embroidering them.

At last their wares were completed, and

sent in, to the great exultation of Mrs. Lacquer and equal admiration of the lady-committee, who unanimously declared that the Misses Lacquers' stall would be the most attractive, and confer the greatest benefit upon the treasury of the association—whose sole end was charity. But those good Christians never gave a thought to the number of consumptive heart-broken girls who were struggling for a slender livelihood—in many cases to support others besides themselves—by manufacturing the very same kind of things offered at the fancy-fair, with the exception of their being better made and much cheaper than the amateur articles. Or it they did once think about it, the only feeling was in all probability one of vanity, in being able to compete with regular manufacturers, without having been brought up to labour And of course the Honourable Kensington Pump would sooner wear a pair of gaudy braces painted upon velvet by the fair

hands of Miss Lacquer herself, and exhibit
them at water-parties, or other occasions on
which he had to take off his coat in public,

than a pair of the same kind ornamented by
nobody knew who, and bought at a bazaar.
How could any one expect it would be otherwise ; although a bewitching smile of thanks was
all the change he got for his five-pound note ?
And young Fitzmoses also, who had all the incli-
nation and none of the ability to become a man
about town, did not at all grumble at buying a
guinea pen-wiper for the purposes of charity ;
it was such a rare chance, also, to get the oppor-
tunity of "chaffing" the refined daughters of
the west end, whilst making the purchase,
just as if they had been common stall-keepers
at the counters of the Pantheon or Soho
Bazaar.   This was very pleasant and agreeable
to all parties, heightened by the good they felt
they were doing in a benevolent point of view.
It was impossible to benefit everybody, and
although every article that was sold took a
crust from the board of some industrious
female artist, yet it swelled the treasury of the

" Ladies'-babies'-bib-and-tucker-general-loan-association," and the various young ladies who kept the stalls were so much delighted with the public exhibition of their own wares and attractions—so gratified at the compliments paid to both by the gentlemen purchasers—including even the officers who had so liberally allowed the band of their regiment to play upon the occasion ; but who, however, did not buy a great many things—that they almost hoped the funds of the society would get into an embarrassed state once more, that they might again have the pleasure of assisting them

And, finally, Mrs. Lacquer and her daughters, when all was over, and they had received the especial thanks of the committee for their exertions, agreed there were many social virtues to be exercised by all right-thinking and religious people, but that the greatest of these was Charity.

CHAPTER VIII.

~~~~~~~

MRS SPANGLE LACQUER'S COUNTRY CONNEXION.

A SISTER of Mrs Lacquer's married a gentleman of property, and resides in the country. Her name is Mrs. ChampignonStiffback, which betrays the foreign origin of her husband, although he is himself an Englishman.

They are tolerable specimens of high rural gentility.

The Stiffbacks reside in a village about two or three miles from a country town, which they make their metropolis. They visit London occasionally during the season, when they usually stay with the Lacquers, and pick up a few fresh notions to astonish the rustics. But beyond this they are not very fond of town. They perceive they are not there of sufficient importance, and they prefer being the storks amongst an assembly of rural frogs, to the unheeded nobodies of a great city. Not, however, that they are always perfectly at their ease in the country; for their position is somewhat uncomfortably poised between the real county aristocracy and the petty agricultural gentilities, belonging to neither, and occasionally looked shy at by both. And since they are in perpetual fear of losing *caste* in the frigid respectability of these districts, by an unlucky acquaintance or an unfortunate slight, their existence is a continuous scene of anxious manœuvring and *finesse;* making strict search into the origin and position of all people taking houses in their vicinity, whom they hang off from calling upon, until they have ascertained who and what their new neighbours are. And in country visiting, it is absolutely necessary to find out all those ladies and gentlemen who do not meet each other, either from natural antipathy, touchy disposition, or fancied difference of rank; by means of which knowledge alone rural dinner-parties can be satisfactorily arranged, to the equal comfort of the host or hostess and their visitors, who would otherwise be obliged to sit looking at each other, like fighting cats, across the table. And this cautious manner of proceeding gives an impetus to country visiting, instead of restraining it. For example, the A.'s have a party, and ask the B.'s and C.'s. The B.'s next invite the other two families, and then the C.'s ask the A.'s and B.'s in company with the D.'s. And finally, the last-named persons return the hospitality of the C.'s., excluding, of course, the others; but asking the E.'s and F.'s in their places, to show that they can command quite as good a circle of society.

As with their relatives in town, the Stiffbacks made religion the principal medium for exhibiting their gentility to the eyes of the world. But it is obliged to be managed in a different manner, since in a country village there is no fashionable church wherein to blazon forth plumes and cachmeres to a patrician audience—for audience is in this case a far more natural word than congregation. The humble fane receives alike the peasant and the aristocrat; and the preacher must make his discourse equally intelligible to both, instead of seeking by theatrical declamation and high-flown language to secure the affections of the

higher class alone—the chief object of the
London Pet Parson.   And so, as distinction
is not to be obtained by attending church,
the Stiffbacks belong to what is termed
a "District Society," for visiting the poor at
their own houses.   This is not for the purpose
of distributing beef and blankets to the hungry
and naked, but for the far more laudable design
of consoling the sick and starving with a tract,
which they are requested to read, keep clean,

and then return And conjoined to this society
Mrs. Stiffback, in company with some other
ladies, has established a private Sunday-school,
wherein some fifteen or twenty fidgety children
study "Reading made Uneasy" in a hot, ill-
ventilated room on fine summer afternoons,
and sing hymns that would drive even Hullah
mad—in which they evince their gratitude
to their benefactors by frequent yawns and
shuffles, and longing glances at the waving
trees and green pastures about the school-
house. The ladies take it in turns to become
governesses, and all appear to find great delight
in the occupation, except Mrs. Heartly, who
was profane enough one afternoon to give all
the children tea and cake, instead of affording
the usual hebdomadal aliment to their minds—
a proceeding which drew down upon her the
indignation of every pious and well-regulated
individual in the village, including, of course,
Mrs. Stiffback at the head of them, until she

found that Mrs. Heartly was on visiting terms in London with Mrs. Spangle Lacquer—of whom the Stiffbacks think a great deal—when she immediately pronounced it a very charitable and thoughtful benefaction.

Indeed, it was at Mrs. Heartly's instance alone that Mrs. Stiffback refrained from paying a visit to Widow Hopkins, whither she intended to go and lecture the poor woman upon the impropriety of her allowing her children to have the measles, and actually staying away from church one Sunday to attend upon them, when the infant was also taken ill. Not, however, that Mrs. Stiffback felt much affection for Mrs. Heartly in reality, nor did any of her friends; for whilst they themselves were in the habit of dressing more expensively than others in the village—in fact, visited London, almost expressly for the purpose of bringing down the newest fashions—still the Heartlys were upon most intimate terms with many of the county fami-

lies, who only received Mrs. Stiffback and her
party with the formality of cold politeness
And this was the more remarkable, because although the Heartlys were really well-born, yet
their income was somewhat limited; and both
mother and daughters went about in common
whittles and straw-bonnets, which Mrs. Stiffback would scarcely have allowed her nursery-
maid to wear—certainly not her governess.
But after all, the Heartlys were very peculiar
in their habits.

Mr. Stiffback may be briefly described as
one of that large body of *parvenus* who have
lost the civility of the tradesman, without ac-
quiring the manners of the gentleman. He
walks about the village as if every pebble and
blade of grass was under subjection to him,
and is courteous to no one—being pompous
even to his equals, and taking no notice of his
superiors—possibly for the simple reason that
they are not particularly attentive to him. He

makes the village coach take him round to his own door—why, it is difficult to determine, for he pays no more than anybody else; but he thinks this gives him consequence, and so he enforces it.

Independent of those in that sphere of visiting which they are pleased to term their own, the Stiffbacks court the professional society of the village. The clergyman of course comes first; and he is at all times most polite to his entertainers, because they always head the coal and missionary subscriptions, and are indefatigable in collecting penny-pieces for the conversion of anonymous savages living in unknown islands. Besides, Mr. Stiffback had the weathercock of the church re-gilt at his own expense. Then comes the medical man, and then the lawyer. This last gentleman believes himself to be the link between the upper and lower orders in the neighbourhood; but as his clients contain some of either class, he is necessarily obliged to be polite to both, and give occasional dinners; but these dinners are always in sets of graduated distinction. And although he sometimes appears to slight his less important connexions, yet they do not take much notice of it; for they are aware that he goes into better society than they do—that if they offended him the others would still receive him; and so, for the sake of scratching together a little important society, they pocket all sorts of affronts, which would be revenged upon an equal or inferior with unmitigated severity.

CHAPTER IX.

"THE LATEST INTELLIGENCE."

FOR A long time we saw very little of the Lacquers, or any of their connexions— principally because we did not care to pay any extra-attention to a set of people who had so few feelings in common with ourselves. We are perfectly aware that the heart, even in its proper state, is simply a hollow muscle; but this organ, in all the Lacquer family, was so very cavernous, that it almost resembled a human drum, making a loud, empty noise to the world from its very hollowness, but destitute of any sympathy with its fellows.

Now and then, however, we saw the name of "Spangle Lacquer, Esq." amongst the advertised directors of some new Improvident Assurance Society, or in a file of aristocratic subscriptions. Then the fashionable newspapers contrived occasionally to make a paid paragraph look as unlike an advertisement as possible, in heralding forth the description of a *féte* or *soirée* given by the lady; and after that we heard vague reports that one of the daughters was about to marry a foreign nobleman—Count or Baron Somebody or another, whom we had seen flitting about Hanway Yard and Regent Street. Like his compatriot *flâneurs*, he was of seedy appearance, and always awakened a wish in you to shave him, cut his hair, and plunge him into

a warm bath. Indeed, we once saw his attention fixed at a placard outside a fur-shop in one of the thoroughfares just named; and when we read the announcement of "*Foreign skins cleaned here,*" we thought what great advantages the establishment could offer to many of the Continentalists who crowd our pavements.

Subsequently the match was off; and people said he behaved very badly. For our own part, we think his conduct was strictly honourable; inasmuch as when he heard that the father lived up to his income, and did not mean to give his daughters anything until he died, the foreign nobleman with a fine sense of feeling declined dragging Miss Lacquer into a state of poverty—his own property being curiously minute, and worthy of forming an interesting object for the oxyhydrogen microscope at the Polytechnic Institution.

As regarded both the young ladies, affairs were beginning to get desperate, and the usual round of expensive marine boarding-houses was recommended. Here they commenced their attacks upon all the corpulent bachelors with curled hair—the wild young celibataires of five-and-forty, who flourish at those matrimonial

exchanges every autumn—but their success was
not equivalent to their efforts.   After this they
tried what the Opera would do, reckoning upon

the visits of any eligible young men they might
know in the house to their box. But when the
young men came, they were always more intent
upon what the Lacquer girls called " those
impudent dancers," than attentive to the young
ladies ; so this plan was a failure. And finally,
disgusted at the want of taste shown by their
countrymen, they persuaded the heads of their
family to go to Paris, where we again met them,
living in the most expensive hotel of the dearest
quartier, and feeling great pleasure in paying
twice as much as they ought for everything they
purchased, to the great benefit of poor folks
like ourselves who came after them. They
stopped at Paris some little time, and then went
to Switzerland and Italy. Afterwards, somebody met them on the Rhine, and at last they
returned back to England, laden with cart loads
of more alabaster ornaments, German glasses,
and wonderful productions from every place they
had visited, which, we imagine, must convert

their already crowded drawing-rooms into a species of private bazaar. They could have purchased all these things at an equally cheap rate in England, including duty and carriage, but then the chance would have been lost of saying, " We brought that from Florence," or, " When we were at Vienna," and the like speeches. Young Lacquer, whose continental gatherings were confined to an enormous pipe, and some foreign jewellery, was himself always talking of them. The last time we met him, we believe that we offended him beyond reconciliation. He was, as usual, descanting upon his Geneva watch, his Venetian rings, his Florentine mosaic broach, and other articles, when we exhibited a knife which we had purchased at Wolverhampton : and added, after he had announced his intention of visiting Greece next year, that we thought ourselves of spending the summer at Birmingham. He never took any notice of us again, and since then, we have

ceased to visit the family. Our ideas are far too low and common for the refined circles we should meet at their house.

CHAPTER X.

HAVING thus intro duced the Spangle Lacquers to your notice, we are going to bid them farewell. Possibly you may some day come across them They form but one specimen of a class comprising thousands, who appear to think that money alone is necessary to attain distinction in the great world ; and that an almost slavish compliance with the most fiddle-faddle conventions of fashion can alone ensure to them an eligible station in society.

We admit with sorrow that the prototypes of the Spangle Lacquers form the greater portion of the middling circles ; and we have endeavoured in the preceding sketches, if they were too blinded by their own lustre to see it themselves, at all events to show to others the hollow motives which rule so many of our acquaintances in their social ceremonies. And we fear all this will continue until people visit only those whom they really have a regard for, unbiased by show-off interest, or, though last not least, the fear of what other people think. When parties shall be given for the sake of collecting together esteemed friends, instead of displaying plate and crockery, this change will be effected ; but until then, the empty pomp of society towards those whom it affects to honour, will exhibit the same aspect of dreary ostentation as the stand of feathers which the undertaker carries on his head like a tray of pies, does to the corpse it is intended to dignify. For, as we have shown—taking one

entertainment as a specimen of the rest—a
stuck-up dinner-party is one of the most melan
choly examples we can offer of the feudal service by which the givers hold their *caste* in
society Hospitality, which ought to be the
primary cause, is triumphed over by jealousy or
ostentation. The whole entertainment is an
unmitigated series of attempts at rivalry and
display: there is a mute eloquence in every
cover and claret-jug upon the table, which
seems to say, " See in what style we do things
here, compared to your own establishment !"
The premature and sickly vegetables,—per
fectly out of season, but forced and introduced
solely for the gratification of the pleasures of
the purse and pocket of the host, rather than
the palates of the guests,—merely remind us
of the money in the Eastern tale which turned
into leaves ; whilst the dreary conversation
and attempt at *badinage* which pass about the
table, in the constrained style of a horse in

a curb and kicking-strap, with a clog at his heels, have something in them peculiarly distressing. True it is, that after dinner the dialogue becomes somewhat more animated : but then it is the forced excitement of the decanters which effects this change ; and the pleasure derived from it is far different to that we experience from the unrestrained conversation of those real acquaintance who are as warm and animated over a boiled leg of mutton and turnips, as they would be if treated with venison and French beans at Christmas.

MORE FACSIMILE REISSUES
FROM PRYOR PUBLICATIONS

THE NATURAL HISTORY OF STUCK-UP PEOPLE

'We are about to expose, as simply and truthfully as we can, the foolish conventionalities of a large proportion of the middle classes of the present day, who believe that position is attained by climbing up a staircase of moneybags'.

First published 1848   128 pages   Illustrated

ISBN: 0 946014 39 6   Paperback   Publication: August 1995

£3.99

Don't
A Manual of Mistakes and Improprieties more or less prevalent in Conduct and Speech

A best seller in the 1880s and once again in our facsimile edition (over 100,000 copies sold), *Don't* is a reflection of a society long since past, and makes for fascinating and amusing reading now.

112 pages   ISBN: 0 946014 02 7   Paperback

£3.50

ENGLISH AS SHE IS SPOKE
OR A JEST IN SOBER EARNEST

This book derives from Pedro Carolino's 'Guide to the Conversation in Portuguese and English' published in 1869. It shows that Carolino's knowledge of English was little more than that furnished by a French-English dictionary and was a greater contribution to humour than linguistics!

First published 1885   80 pages   ISBN: 0 946014 09 4   Paperback   £3.50

MANNERS FOR MEN

Mrs Humphry, who is also the author of *Manners for Women*, wrote 'Like every other woman I have my ideal of manhood. The difficulty is to describe it. First of all, he must be a gentleman, but that means so much that it, in its turn, requires explanation . . .'

First published 1897   176 pages
ISBN: 0 946014 23 X   Paperback

£4.50

MANNERS FOR WOMEN

Can anything be nicer than a really nice girl? 'may seem quaint but it is a useful reminder that tittering is an unpleasant habit and curtesying should be avoided unless you know what you are doing.' *The Times.*

First published 1897   164 pages
ISBN: 0 946014 17 5   Paperback

£3.95

What Shall I Say?

A guide to letter writing for ladies first published in 1898.
132 pages   ISBN: 0 946014 25 6   Paperback

£3.50

MASTER YOUR MOODS

Subtitled 'Philosophy for Daily Life' quotations from writers including Bacon, Socrates and Dr Johnson will help when you are feeling anger, worry, envy or just about any other emotion.

First published 1885   64 pages   ISBN: 0 946014 34 5   Paperback

£3.50

A SHORT HISTORY OF THE WOLF IN BRITAIN

Taken from James Harting's 'British Animals Extinct Within Modern Times', first published in 1880, here are early accounts of the wolf in the British Isles until its demise around 1760.

96 pages   Illustrated   ISBN: 0 946014 27 2   Paperback

£5.95

OUR NATIVE ENGLAND
BEING THE HISTORY OF ENGLAND MADE EASY

For each ruler from Egbert to Victoria, and also including tribes from the
Britons to Jutes and Angles, this little book instructs and informs with
woodcuts and brief descriptions in rhyme.

First published 1838   64 pages   47 woodcuts

ISBN: 0 946014 19 1   Paperback

£2.99

HAND SHADOWS

A delightful resurrection of an amusing and educational pastime now sadly
neglected — the perfect antidote to today's rush and bustle.

First published 1860   48 pages   Illustrated

ISBN: 0 946014 24 8   Paperback

£3.99

SPECTROPIA
OR SURPRISING SPECTRAL ILLUSIONS SHOWING GHOSTS EVERYWHERE

It is difficult here to believe that our eyes are not deceiving us, as ghosts and other images such
as Mr Punch and a rainbow appear — and in colour! No technical knowledge or apparatus is
needed. Follow the simple instructions and be amazed!

First published 1863   48 pages   Colour and other
Illustrations   ISBN: 0 946014 31 0   Paperback

£4.99

WHY NOT EAT INSECTS?

'My congratulations to Pryor Publications for keeping this little classic in print so that more
generations can be entertained, enthralled and educated.' David Bellamy.

First published 1885   104 pages

ISBN: 0 946014 12 4   Paperback

£3.50

Available from bookshops or post free from
PRYOR PUBLICATIONS
75 Dargate Road, Yorkletts, Whitstable, Kent CT5 3AE, England.
Tel. & Fax: (01227) 274655
A full list of our publications sent free on request